I0797668

Gross Stuff!

Gross Stuff in History

by Julie Murray

Dash!
LEVELED READERS
An Imprint of Abdo Zoom • abdobooks.com

Level 1 – Beginning
Short and simple sentences with familiar words or patterns for children who are beginning to understand how letters and sounds go together.

Level 2 – Emerging
Longer words and sentences with more complex language patterns for readers who are practicing common words and letter sounds.

Level 3 – Transitional
More developed language and vocabulary for readers who are becoming more independent.

abdobooks.com

Published by Abdo Zoom, a division of ABDO, PO Box 398166, Minneapolis, Minnesota 55439.

Dash!™ is a trademark and logo of Abdo Zoom.

Printed in the United States of America, North Mankato, Minnesota.
052025
092025

Photo Credits: Alamy, Getty Images, Shutterstock
Production Contributors: Jennie Forsberg, Grace Hansen, John Hansen
Design Contributors: Candice Keimig, Neil Klinepier

Library of Congress Control Number: 2024947664

Publisher's Cataloging in Publication Data

Names: Murray, Julie, author.
Title: Gross stuff in history / by Julie Murray
Description: Minneapolis, Minnesota : Abdo Zoom, 2026 | Series: Gross stuff! | Includes online resources and index.
Identifiers: ISBN 9781098288631 (lib. bdg.) | ISBN 9781098289331 (ebook) | ISBN 9781098289683 (Read-to-me ebook)
Subjects: LCSH: Cleanliness--Juvenile literature. | History--Juvenile literature. | Human body--Care and hygiene--Juvenile literature. | Refuse and refuse disposal--Juvenile literature. | Sanitation--Juvenile literature. | Curiosities and wonders--Juvenile literature.
Classification: DDC 904--dc23

Table of Contents

Gross Stuff in History

History is events from the past. Humans study history. The things we learn from the past can be interesting, while others are downright gross!

drying
wrapping

The ancient Egyptians lived thousands of years ago. They mummified their dead. First, they removed the body's **organs**. Then, they dried the body and wrapped it in linen cloths. Bodies that went through this process can still be seen today.

Cannibalism dates back more than 1.4 million years! It could be a religious **ritual** or a necessity. The Donner Party was a group of **pioneers** who lived in the 1800s. They had to be cannibals to survive.

Medical Practices

One of the earliest surgical **procedures** was trepanation. It involved cutting or drilling a hole into someone's skull. It was done to relieve pressure. It was also believed to release evil spirits.

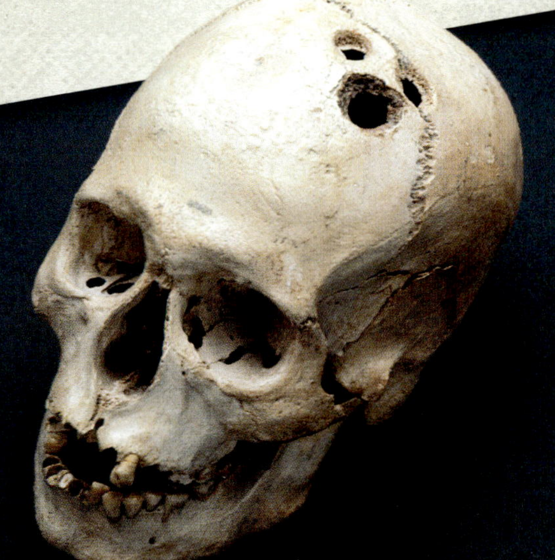

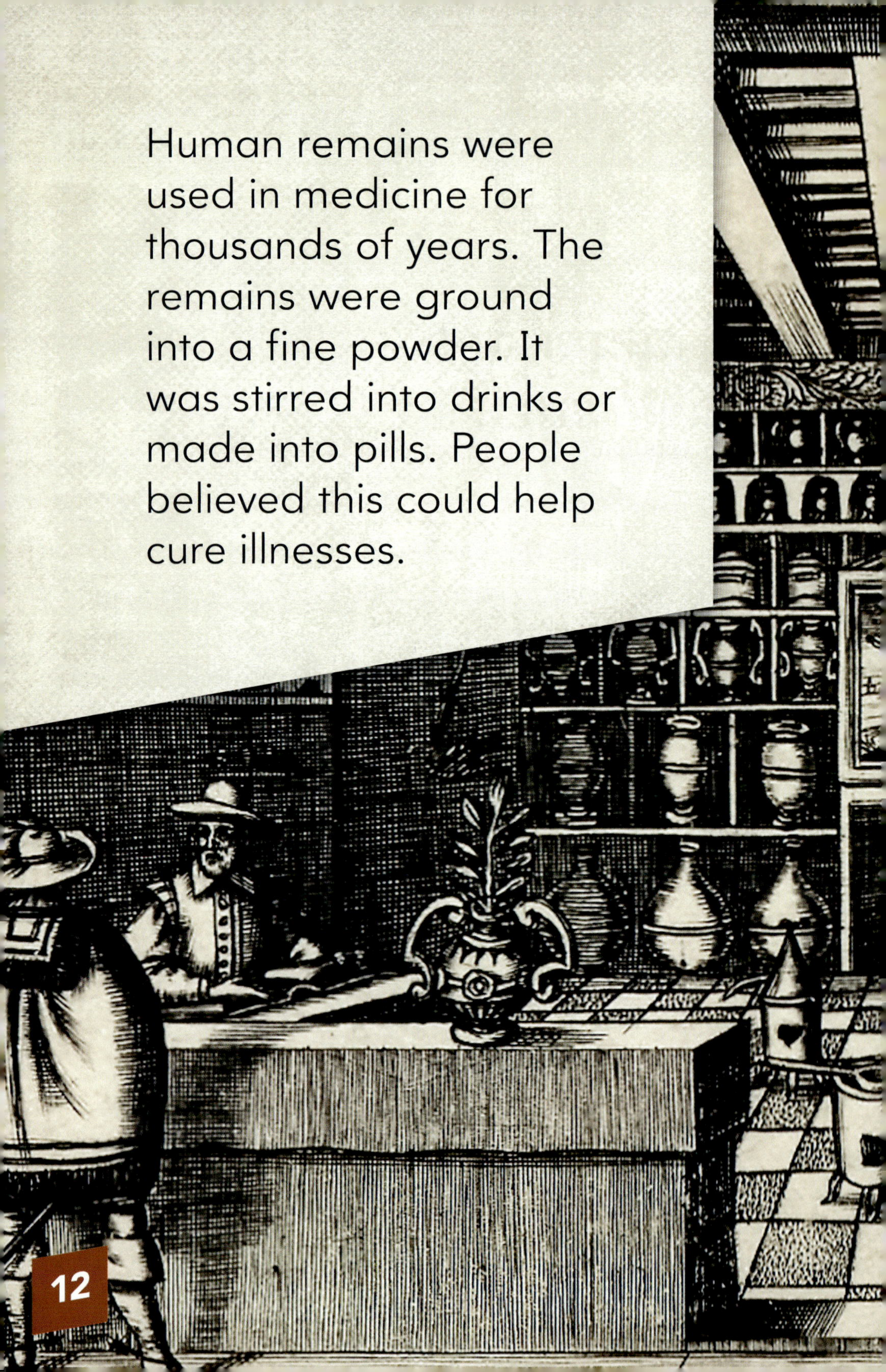

Human remains were used in medicine for thousands of years. The remains were ground into a fine powder. It was stirred into drinks or made into pills. People believed this could help cure illnesses.

13

On June 15, 1815, thousands of soldiers lost their lives in the Battle of Waterloo. The teeth of the dead soldiers were sold to dentists. The teeth were used to make **dentures**.

Animal dung was once used to treat medical issues. Elephant poop was used for headaches. Pig poop was used to stop nosebleeds. Cow poop was used to treat arthritis.

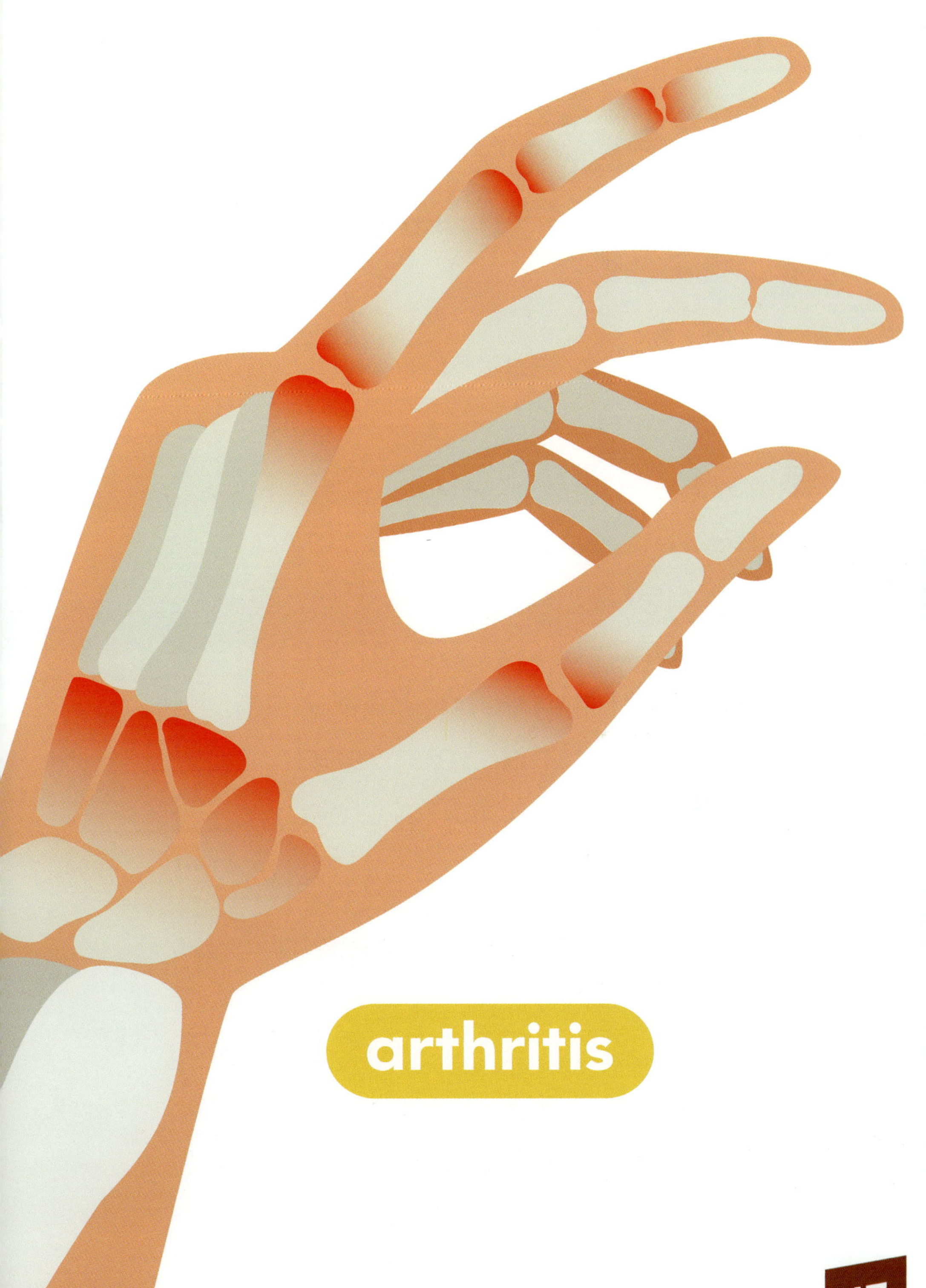

arthritis

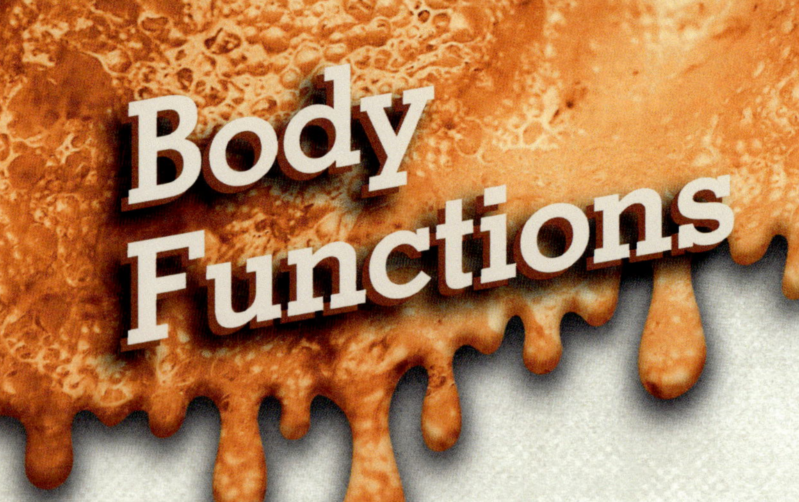

Body Functions

The ancient Romans used pee as mouthwash. It was believed to get rid of germs and whiten teeth. Pee was also collected and used as laundry soap to clean clothes!

People in Europe used to get rid of bodily waste through slides that went to the street. **Chamber pots** were also dumped out of windows. This created a stinky mess and unclean conditions.

More Facts

- Women used to wear live insects for fashion. The insects would be placed in a small cage. Then, they were pinned to clothing.

- Many strange cures for baldness have been used throughout history. One was to rub horseradish and pigeon poop on the head.

- Toothpaste was once made of gross ingredients. Lizard livers and mashed-up mice were often used. Crushed bones and oyster shells were sometimes used too!

Glossary

cannibalism – the act of eating human flesh by a human being.

chamber pot – a small, portable, pot-shaped receptacle for urine and other waste, usually kept in a bedroom.

denture – a partial or complete set of artificial teeth.

organ – a part of the body that performs a particular task. The heart, lungs, and brain are all examples of organs.

pioneer – a person or group that explores new areas.

procedure – a series of actions performed by a doctor to treat a medical condition.

ritual – a set form for going through the steps of a religious ceremony.

Index

Online Resources

To learn more about gross stuff in history, please visit **abdobooklinks.com** or scan this QR code. These links are routinely monitored and updated to provide the most current information available.